LIBRARY
California School for the Deaf
Riverside

D0599533

Viva Mexico!

The
Folk
Arts

George Ancona

BENCHMARK BOOKS

MARSHALL CAVENDISH
NEW YORK

To Darby McQuade

Gracias to the people who helped
make this book: Irene Aguilar,
Braulio Alonzo Ruiz and his family,
Gabriel Aristide Montoto,
the Fuentes family, Conchita Garval,
Emilio and Miguel Quintana,
Pedro Reyes Júarez,
Genoveva Rosales Lopez.

Benchmark Books
Marshall Cavendish Corporation
99 White Plains Road
Tarrytown, NY 10591-9001
Website: www.marshallcavendish.com
Copyright © 2002 by George Ancona
All rights reserved. No part of this book may
be reproduced in any form without written
permission from the publisher.

Library of Congress Cataloging-in-Publication Data
Ancona, George.
The folk arts / by George Ancona.
p. cm. — (Viva Mexico!)
Includes index.
ISBN 0-7614-1326-X
1. Folk art—Mexico—Juvenile literature. [1. Folk
art—Mexico.] I. Title. II. Series.
NK844.A53 2001   745'.0972—dc21   00-053018

Printed in Hong Kong

6 5 4 3 2

Contents

Colorful Mexico

Mexico is a country full of color. Fields and forests and waters are splashed with the strong hues of a warm climate. Markets explode with the bright oranges, reds, and greens of fruits and vegetables. Mexicans celebrate color through the many beautiful objects they make.

The arts can be seen not only in museums but on the streets of towns and cities. Walls are painted with strong colors, and murals sing out the stories of Mexico. People wear traditional clothing with intricate patterns that tell us where they come from.

Mexicans create art from the materials they find around them. They mold clay, carve wood, paint, weave, sew, form metal, and cut paper. Then they pass these beautiful objects to others who make them part of their lives. Through their arts they tell the world who they are.

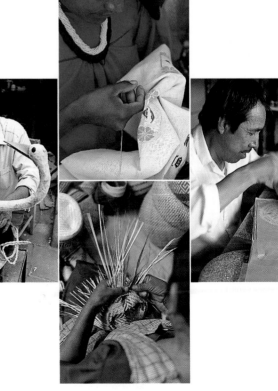

Stone

The ancient peoples of Mexico left behind the ruins of imposing cities and temples covered with powerful stone carvings. Buried in the rubble were jewelry, pottery, and decorations—a legacy of great civilizations that speaks to and inspire artists today.

With the coming of the Spanish in 1519, native cultures were overwhelmed and almost completely destroyed. Temples were dismantled, and their stones were used to raise churches. At first, during Mexico's colonial period, churches looked like forts. Their exterior walls were massive and plain. In the seventeenth century, during the baroque period, the facades and interiors blossomed with the carvings of native artists and artisans. These works, commissioned by religious orders and wealthy families, gave new expression to churches and mansions.

Wood

Baroque churches were filled with wooden carvings, which were covered with gold leaf, thin sheets of gold glued to the wood. Originally, wooden statues were brought from Spain. But Mexican wood carvers quickly mastered the Spanish techniques and created a new form of expression, that of the Mexican image.

Forests provided the hard and soft woods for carving intricate doors and for making very fine furniture. Wooden utensils— serving spoons and beaters called *molinillos* used to mix hot chocolate—are still found in Mexican kitchens.

Today in some towns, entire families work together to create wooden carvings of animals and fantastic creatures called *alebrijes*. After school and during vacations, children work as apprentices to their elders. Many of their carvings are sent to other countries, where they are collected and held in great esteem.

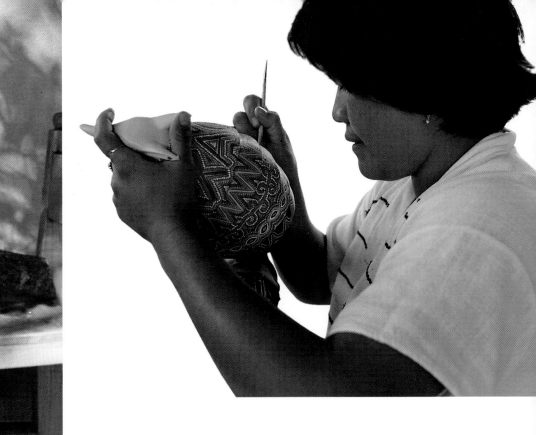

The men gather the wood and carve the figures; the women paint the details with brilliant color.

Masks. No festival would be complete without the fantasy created by masks. Master carvers are important members of towns, which celebrate their feast days with dances and pageants. A client goes to the mask maker and orders a very specific mask that will disguise him and complete his costume. Masks are expensive, and often a father or uncle will pass his on to a young dancer. Masks are made not only of wood but of wire mesh, papier-mâché, cloth, or any material that is appropriate.

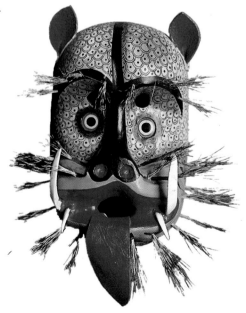

Metal

Blacksmiths, sculptors, jewelers, and metalworkers use all types of metals—gold, silver, iron, copper, bronze, and tin. Bronze statues are at the center of the fountains in *zócalos* (town squares). Children play and sit on whimsical sculptures in the parks. Buildings almost always have intricate wrought-iron railings, gates, and window guards.

14

Jewelry. Uppermost in the minds of the Spanish who invaded Mexico was their desire for gold. The native people greeted them as if they were gods and presented them with gifts of gold, silver, and copper jewelry. The Spanish soon found the mines that held the precious metals, and then forced the Indians to work in them. The mines not only provided wealth for the Spanish treasury but also the materials to make finely worked jewelry. Today the women from Tehuantepec in southwest Mexico display their gold jewelry at fiestas. Filigreed gold earrings frame their faces, and necklaces of gold hang heavily on embroidered blouses and skirts.

Fabric

Weaving is an ancient art that continues today. A fragment
of pre-Columbian weaving has been dated back to around
1800 B.C. Ancient weavers used cotton and sisal (from the
leaves of the agave plant). The Spanish introduced sheep to
Mexico, which provided native weavers with a new fiber:
wool. Today there are weavers who still use natural dyes to

weave beautiful rugs. Some weavers use a back-strap loom to weave narrow fabrics and sashes.

In the more tropical regions, most people sleep in hammocks to keep cool. The Spanish discovered that the Indians of the West Indies used hammocks and introduced them to the Mexicans. Hammocks are woven with colorful string.

El Rebozo. The *rebozo* is the traditional shawl worn by Mexican women. They wear it in different ways. They wrap or pile it on their heads to keep off the sun or to make a pad to carry a bundle. It is wrapped around the shoulders for warmth or over the head and shoulders. They also carry their babies in *rebozos*, in front when they nurse or on their back. Inside a church, women cover their heads with their *rebozos*. (In Tehuantepec, though, women wear lace headdresses in churches and at dances.)

Embroidery. To the ancient Mexican, clothing was very important. It showed the social level to which a person belonged. Weaving cotton was women's work. Today homespun fabrics are giving way to machine-made cloth, but hand embroidery is still used to decorate garments. Each region has its own traditional dress and designs.

The ancient *huipil* is still worn by women in the warmer

areas of Mexico, such as Yucatan. It is a loose-fitting white
dress with embroidery around the collar and sleeves. On
feast days women put on formal huipils decorated with
embroidery and lace. It can take a year to embroider
such a dress.

Men wear fine white straw hats with shirts called
guayaberas, pants, and sandals to dance in.

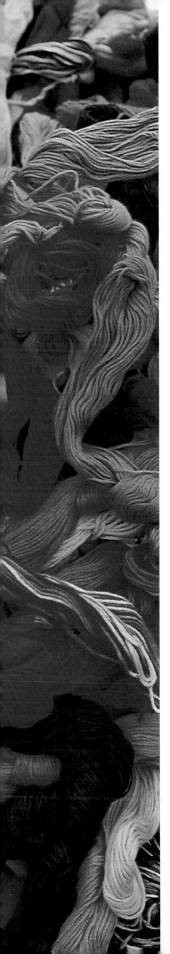

Yarn. The Huichol people from the north use colorful yarns to decorate their fabrics. Women sew shapes and patterns on cloth using little Xs called cross-stitching. Fabric dolls have faces made with cross-stitched designs. Men wear cross-stitched or woven shoulder bags. Yarns are pressed into soft beeswax to make intricate pictures depicting Huichol legends. And colored yarns in wax also decorate wooden masks and animal carvings.

Clay

Ceramics is an art that has come down through the centuries from the time of the early farming villages. Pots were made for carrying water, for cooking, and for storing food. After the conquest, European and Asian ways of decorating pottery were adopted by native potters. Potters began to use the wheel to shape pots, which they then glazed. Different regions developed their own styles. Ceramic pots, dishes, and tiles are found today in kitchens throughout Mexico. And these clay products are exported to many corners of the world.

Potters turn clay into dishes, pots, and vases on rotating wheels. In Talavera ceramics from Puebla, pots are painted with glazes after a first firing. Then the pottery is fired again. The intense heat in the kiln fuses the colors into the clay. The pots come out transformed. The colors are brighter, and the clay now has a hard, shiny surface. Tiles are also made in this way and are used to protect and decorate the walls of buildings and the domes of churches.

The Mexican's sense of humor is reflected in colorful clay figures that portray ordinary people in their daily lives. Families devote themselves to making these figures and often have a store attached to their workshop for selling their crafts. From the shop, visitors can watch the family working at their various tasks. Their works can also be found in marketplaces and shops around the world.

Straw

Gathering reeds in marshes, leaves from palm trees, and twigs in forests, Mexicans weave baskets of all shapes and sizes. Woven animals and figures are used as toys and decorations. A Mayan family dyes palms to weave toy cars, airplanes, and animals. Swift, nimble fingers also weave colored strips into baskets and purses.

Beads

The Huichol people still live in their traditional ways in remote areas. They have developed their own way of using glass beads. With these beads they patiently create spectacular jewelry, such as necklaces from which a square beaded ornament hangs. They also decorate animal figures, masks, and bowls with designs made of beads. They spread softened beeswax over the objects and press the beads into it. When the wax cools, the beads are fixed in place.

Toys

A child exploring the shops in a market will discover a wonderland of toys and miniature dishes, pretend food, and furniture for dollhouses. There are tin soldiers, circus acrobats, cars, and trucks. Dolls are made from an endless variety of materials. Fabric, straw, palm leaves, cornhusks, bamboo, rags, yarn, wood, and papier-mâché become figures in the hands of skilled doll makers. Two corks, a few feathers, and some paper on the end of wires become two roosters fighting. Tiny furniture, pots, and pans allow children to lose themselves in a world of their own making.

Paper

Papel Picado. Mexican artists and craftspeople spend many hours making something that will disappear in a few seconds. Fireworks, piñatas, and *papel picados* are only a few examples.

A fiesta is announced with *papel picados*. These are sheets of colored tissue paper with images stamped out on them, which are strung together across streets, plazas, or rooms. In a small town a master paper cutter and his daughter punch out images in tissue paper. Plastic sheets are also used. They last longer, but they cost more.

Papier-Mâché. When paper is soaked in a paste made by cooking flour in water, the paper turns into papier-mâché. When pasted over a split bamboo frame in the shape of a bull, it becomes a *torito*, the bull that carries the fireworks during fiestas. Papier-mâché can also be shaped into realistic and colorful fruits, vegetables, and breads. These shapes are covered with lacquer to protect the paper.

For the Day of the Dead, when families honor their dead loved ones, skeletons are made to look as if they are doing things that living people do. This is the Mexican's way of making fun of death. Papier-mâché is also plastered over split bamboo forms to make giant puppets. At parties, boys put on the papier-mâché puppets and dance, making the puppets seem to come alive.

Piñatas. And best of all, papier-mâché is used to make the piñatas for children to break on their birthdays. Piñatas can be clowns, animals, birds, trains, cars—almost anything that can hold candies, fruits, and small toys.

Each child at a party has a turn at trying to break the swinging piñata with a stick while the others sing:

Dale, dale, dale,	Hit it, hit it, hit it
No pierdas el tino,	Don't lose your aim,
Mide la distancia,	Measure the space,
Vas por buen camino.	You're doing fine.

When the piñata breaks, the treats rain down, and everyone scrambles to gather as many as they can. And so another beautiful work of art disappears, but in its short life it has given pleasure to many.

Make a Piñata

A piñata can be made with a balloon. Use it for any round or oval shape—like a fish.

Attach cardboard fins, gills, and a tail to the balloon with masking tape.

Pour a tablespoon of flour and a cup of water into a pot. With the help of an adult, heat over a low flame, stirring until the mixture thickens. Remove from the heat and let it cool. Tear newspapers into strips and dip them into the paste.

Lay the strips across the balloon and the cardboard fins. Lips can be shaped with the wet paper. Build up to about four layers, allowing each layer to dry before adding another. Add a piece of cardboard where you will make the holes for the string to hang it.

Paint the dry piñata white. Then use colors to decorate or paste colored tissue paper for scales. Paste thin strips of tissue paper to the fins. Run two cords through the piñata, front and back, to hang it level. Cut a door on top, fill the piñata and tape it shut. Now go break it!

46

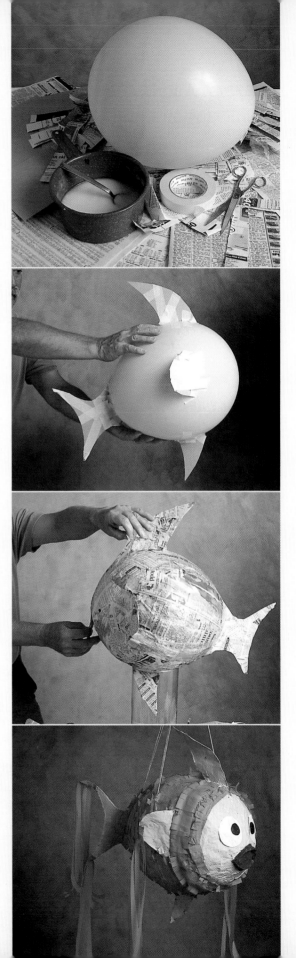

Glossary

Words in italics are Spanish words in this book.

alebrije   wooden carving
cross-stitch   sewing in which stitches form Xs
embroidery   patterns stitched into material
façade   face, or outside wall of a building
fiesta   festival (from the Spanish word, *fiesta*)
filigree   ornamental work of fine gold, silver, or copper wire
gold leaf   thin sheet of gold
guayabera   man's shirt
Huichol   Indians in northern Mexico
huipil   loose-fitting white dress with embroidery
inlaid   design set into a surface
molinillo   beater
papel picado   cut-out paper
papier-mâché   paper soaked in a paste
piñata   papier-mâché shape filled with candy
rebozo   shawl
Talavera   style of pottery from Puebla
Tehuantepec   town in southwest Mexico
torito   papier-mâché bull
wrought iron   tough, soft iron that can be shaped
zócalo   town square

Find out More

Garza, Carmen Lomas. *Making Magic Windows: Creating Papel Picado*. San Francisco: Childrens Book Press, 1999.

Harris, Zoe and Susan Williams. *Piñatas & Smiling Skeletons*. Berkeley, California: Pacific View Press, 1998.

Masuoka, Susan N. *En Calavera: The Papier-Mâché Art of the Linares Family*. Los Angeles, California: UCLA Fowler Museum of Cultural History, 1994.

Milord, Susan. Mexico! *40 Activities to Experience Mexico Past and Present*. Charlotte, Vermont: Williamson Publishing Company, 1998.

Perl, Lila. *Piñatas and Paper Flowers: Holidays of the Americas in English and Spanish*. Madison, Wisconsin: Demco, 1983.

Index

Page numbers for illustrations are in boldface

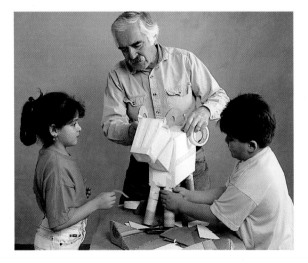

About the Author

George Ancona has made piñatas for all of his six children's birthdays. Now that they have grown up, he is making them for his grandchildren and his friends. That's a lot of piñatas! The only complaint his grandchildren have is that the piñatas he makes are too pretty to break. So now he makes them with a door that is pulled open with a string. This way, the children have the goodies and save the piñata.